D1386951

HOTCHPOTCH

Do you know how many men can be
shaved in 60 minutes?
Who can't you marry?
Which is the most spoken language in
the world?
Make your own model Lifeboat Man.
Do you know how to make Welsh
Rarebit?
Follow the **HOTCHPOTCH MAN** –
and enjoy yourself...

3 bcd

Other books by GYLES BRANDRETH

DOMINO GAMES AND PUZZLES
NUMBER GAMES AND PUZZLES
GAMES AND PUZZLES WITH COINS AND MATCHES
PAPER AND PENCIL GAMES AND PUZZLES
ROYAL QUIZ BOOK

and published by CAROUSEL BOOKS

Gyles Brandreth

HOTCHPOTCH

Illustrated by Ann Axworthy

CAROUSEL BOOKS
A DIVISION OF TRANSWORLD PUBLISHERS LTD

HOTCHPOTCH

A CAROUSEL BOOK 0 552 54112 5

First publication in Great Britain

PRINTING HISTORY
Carousel edition published 1976
Carousel edition reprinted 1977

Copyright © Gyles Brandreth 1976
Illustrator's copyright © Transworld Publishers Ltd. 1976

Carousel Books are published by
Transworld Publishers Ltd.,
Century House, 61–63 Uxbridge Road,
Ealing, London W5 5SA
Made and printed in Great Britain by
Cox & Wyman Ltd., London, Reading and Fakenham

Start Here

A hotchpotch, according to the biggest dictionary I can find, is 'a dish of many mixed ingredients, especially mutton broth with vegetables'! Well, I'm sorry to have to disappoint you, but if you've bought, borrowed, begged or been given this book expecting to find a delicious bowl of hot broth inside, you're in for a big surprise. There are lots and lots of excellent and extraordinary and exciting things in the pages that follow, but mutton and veg. aren't among them. *This* hotchpotch is a hotchpotch with a difference. Let me begin by giving you a list of the ingredients, so that you can get a taste of things to come and an idea of where to find them:

And on top of all that you'll find a humorous little *Hotchpotch* man dancing about at the top right-hand corner of every other page. I know he looks as if he's standing still, but if you flick through the book at speed you'll find he's dancing merrily all the way. Of course, I'm hoping that by the time you've flicked through the book you'll be dancing merrily too. And even more than that, I'm hoping you will have forgiven me for not giving you mutton broth and vegetables. Next time I will. I promise.

GYLES BRANDRETH.

The World's Most Terrible Tongue-twister

And if you don't believe it, try it ten times in a row:
The Leith police dismisseth us!

Hotchpotch Hinformation

Did you know that you are sharing the earth with an estimated

   3,000,000,000,000,000,000,000,000,000,000,000

other living things?

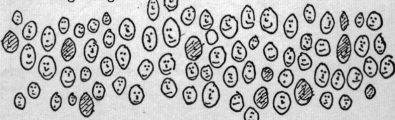

Madelinette

Here is an ancient board game that almost no-one plays nowadays – which is a pity, because it's easy to learn and fascinating to play. It's a game for two players and each player has three counters (coins or shells or sugar lumps or matchboxes or milk-bottle tops will do). The counters are placed on a board that you can draw onto a large sheet of paper and, at the beginning of the game, the counters and the board should look like this:

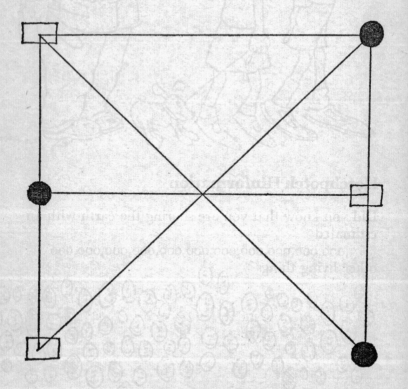

The players toss to see who begins and then take it in turns to move. The first player starts by moving one of his counters along a line to the empty crossing point in the middle of the board. The other player then moves one of his counters along a line to the new empty point. This goes on, with each player moving his counters from point to point one at a time, until one of the players is unable to move any of his counters – when that player has lost.

It's a simple-sounding game, but to master it calls for skill and intelligence.

On a Clear Day

On a clear day you can't see forever, but you can see quite a bit. How far, in fact, you can see depends on how high you are, and the higher you are, the further you can see:

At 5ft you can see 2·9 miles.

At 50ft you can see 9·3 miles.

At 100ft you can see 13·2 miles.

At 1,000ft you can see 41·6 miles.

At 5,000ft you can see 93·1 miles.

At 20,000ft you can see 186·2 miles.

Loony Limerick

A cheerful old bear at the zoo
Could always find something to do.
  When it bored him, you know,
  To walk to and fro,
He reversed it and walked fro and to!

A Twist in the Tale

Sheila's Shetland pony shied,
Shooting Sheila on the shore.
Shaken, Sheila, stupefied,
Struggled homeward, stiff and sore.

Mind-Boggling

Blindfold yourself, give a friend a pencil and a piece of paper and tell him to do exactly as you ask:

1. He must begin by writing down the year of his birth.
2. Under that, he must write any important year in his life.
3. Under that, he must write down the number of years that have passed since the year of his birth and the 'important' year.

4. Under that, get him to write down his present age if he has already had a birthday this year *or* the age he will be at his next birthday if he has not yet had his birthday this year.

5. Now tell him to add up all the figures and, almost before he's had time to do so, tell him the answer is 3952!

As tricks go, this one is fairly impressive. As tricks go, it's also fairly simple! All you are getting your friend to do, after all, is add the present year – 1976 – to itself, because if you add your age to your birth you will get the present year and if you add some year in the past to the number of years that have passed since that year you will again get the present year! In 1976 the answer will always be 1976+1976, which is 3952. In 1977 the answer will be 1977+1977, which is 3954. And so it goes on.

Now you know how it's done, you probably think it's too easy. All the same, try it on a friend or two and see how it baffles them.

Hotchpotch Hilarity

Why is the burglar upstairs an honest man?

Because he is above doing something dishonest!

17

When you've been married for twenty-five years you celebrate your Silver Wedding Anniversary. When you've been married for fifty years you celebrate your Golden Wedding Anniversary. And when you've been married for sixty years you celebrate your Diamond Wedding Anniversary. But when do you celebrate your China Wedding Anniversary? And your Leather Wedding Anniversary? And your Tin Wedding Anniversary? If you know the answers, then you'll find this quiz an easy one, because what you've got to do is match the years on the left to the names on the right. Have a go.

(The answers are on page 113)

One year	Emerald
Two years	Crystal
Three years	Coral
Four years	Cotton
Five years	Bronze
Six years	Sapphire
Seven years	Woollen
Eight years	Ruby
Nine years	Paper
Ten years	Pearl
Fifteen years	Pottery
Twenty years	Tin
Thirty years	Silk
Thirty-five years	Wooden
Forty years	Leather
Forty-five years	China
Fifty-five years	Sweets

Knock, Knock! Who's There?

Knock, knock!
Who's there?
Sam and Janet.
Sam and Janet who?
Some enchanted evening!

Knock, knock!
Who's there?
A little old lady.
A little old lady who?
I didn't know you could
yodel!

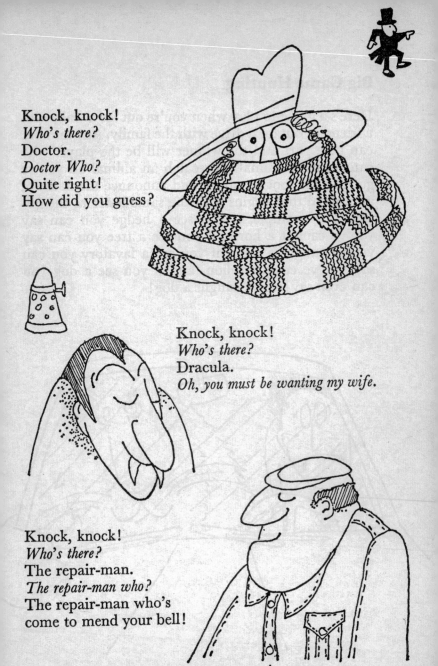

Knock, knock!
Who's there?
Doctor.
Doctor Who?
Quite right!
How did you guess?

Knock, knock!
Who's there?
Dracula.
Oh, you must be wanting my wife.

Knock, knock!
Who's there?
The repair-man.
The repair-man who?
The repair-man who's
come to mend your bell!

Big Game Hunting

Here's a game to play when you're out for a walk with a friend or out for a drive with the family. Any number can take part and the winner will be the player who catches most animals. To catch an animal all you've got to do is spot an object and announce the name of an animal that begins with the same letter as the object. For example, if you see a hedge you can say you've caught a horse, if you see a tree you can say you've caught a tiger, if you see a lavatory you can say you've caught a lion, and if you see a dog you can even say you've caught a dog!

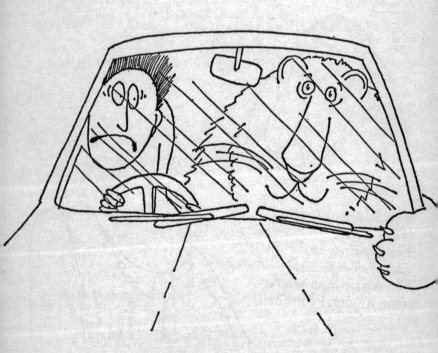

Each item and each animal can only be spotted and caught once, so that when you've seen your hedge and claimed your horse, no one else can use your hedge or have your horse. To catch any more animals beginning with H (a hamster, a hyena, a hedgehog) you will have to spot other things that begin with H (a house, a hill, a hat). As you go along you must keep careful count of the number of animals you've managed to bag and make sure that no two players try to catch the same beast. At the end of the walk or the drive, the player with the largest menagerie has won.

Hotchpotch Hilarity

Why should yellow peas be sent to Hammersmith?

Because that's the way to Turnham Green!

What holds the moon up?

The moon-beams, of course!

Hotchpotch Crossword – the Easy One

Clues Across

1. You could find one of these in the belfry or on the cricket pitch.
2. In the old song this hoppity creature 'would a-wooing go'.
4. In the nursery rhyme about a black sheep, there's a little boy who lives down here.
6. The animal doctor.
7. The opposite of 'against'.
8. When you begin to write a letter you always use this word.
11. This is what Oliver Twist asked for.
12. This four-legged creature has got long ears, a tuft at the end of his tail and is supposed to be very stupid.

Clues Down

1. This snake's a constrictor.
2. This is the name given to a keen football supporter. It's also the name of something that can keep you cool.
3. Sensible people don't play the giddy ——!
4. A Baron is one of these. And so is a Viscount, an Earl and a Duke.
5. And they lived happily —— after.
7. Old Macdonald had one of these.
9. This is a girl's name. And it's also what we call the night before Christmas.
10. These vehicles come in all shapes and sizes, but a double-decker one is best.

(The answers are on page 114)

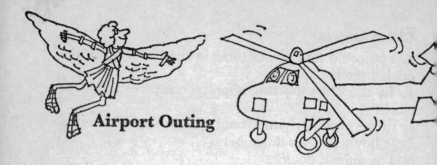

Airport Outing

There's no more fascinating way of spending a day than visiting an airport. It's fun just watching the aircraft land and take off. It's even more fun getting a glimpse behind the scenes. And that's something you can probably arrange by writing a nice letter to the Airport Controller asking if you can come and have a look around. Unless he's very, very busy (and at Heathrow and Gatwick he *is* very, very busy) the chances are he'll write a nice letter back saying 'Yes'. Anyway, it's worth a try.

Here are the names and addresses of the United Kingdom's top twenty-two airports:

ABERDEEN AIRPORT
Dyce, Aberdeen.
ALDERGROVE AIRPORT
Belfast, Northern Ireland.

BIRMINGHAM AIRPORT
Elmdon, Birmingham.
BRISTOL AIRPORT
Lulsgate, Bristol.
EAST MIDLANDS AIRPORT
Castle Donington, Derby.

EXETER AIRPORT
Exeter, Devon.
GATWICK AIRPORT
Horley, Surrey.
GLAMORGAN AIRPORT
Rhoose, Glamorgan.
GLASGOW AIRPORT
Abbotsinch, Renfrewshire.

HEATHROW AIRPORT
Hounslow, Middlesex.
ISLE OF MAN AIRPORT
Ronaldsway, Ballasalla, I.O.M.
JERSEY AIRPORT
States Airport, Jersey, Channel Islands.
LEEDS AIRPORT
Yeadon, Leeds.
LIVERPOOL AIRPORT
Speke, Liverpool.
LUTON AIRPORT
Luton, Bedfordshire.
MANCHESTER AIRPORT
Wythenshawe, Manchester.
NEWCASTLE AIRPORT
Woolsington, Newcastle-upon-
Tyne.

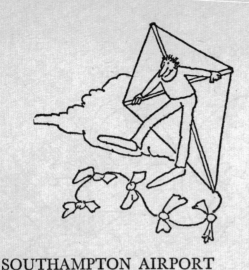

SOUTHAMPTON AIRPORT
Eastleigh, Southampton.
STANSTED AIRPORT
Stansted, Essex.
TEESIDE AIRPORT
Middleton St. George, Darlington, County Durham.
TURNHOUSE AIRPORT
Turnhouse, Edinburgh.
WESTLAND HELIPORT
Lombard Road, London S.W.11.

Where Will You Find It?

1. Where will you find **Lagos**?

   Is it in: Dahomey?
   Niger?
   Uganda?
   Nigeria?

2. Where will you find **Rawalpindi**?

   Is it in: India?
   Pakistan?
   Sri Lanka?
   Bangladesh?

3. Where will you find **Jedda**?

   Is it in: Israel?
   Burma?
   Egypt?
   Saudi Arabia?

Where will you find **Cromer**?
Is it in: Canada?
      Australia?
      England?
      Yugoslavia?
5. Where will you find **Lugano**?
Is it in: Switzerland?
      Italy?
      Belgium?
      Denmark?
6. Where will you find **Zagreb**?
Is it in: Tanzania?
      Yugoslavia?
      Vietnam?
      Chile?

(The answers are on page 114)

Burmese Water Torture

This is one of the world's great practical jokes, but it never fails so choose your victim with care. Begin by standing on a tall chair or a step ladder or anything else that is high enough to enable you to touch the ceiling. Place a glass filled to the brim with water against the ceiling and hold it in position there with the point of a walking stick. Now ask your victim to kindly come over and hold the glass in position by taking the other end of the walking stick while you climb down off the chair or step-ladder. The unfortunate victim obliges, comes over, takes the end of the walking stick and keeps the glass in position by continuing to press it against the ceiling. You now climb down and *take away* the chair or step-ladder, leaving your victim stranded!

Rescue the poor fellow when you've recovered from laughing.

Hotchpotch Hilarity

Which animal drops from the clouds?
    The rain, dear!
Which animal never plays fair?
    The cheetah!
Which animal would you like to be when it's very cold outside?

    A little otter!

Fresh Fried Tongue-twister

What will you have?
 Fried fresh fish?
  Fish fresh fried?
   Fresh fried fish?
    Fresh fish fried?
     Or fish fried fresh?

The Seven Wonders of The Ancient World

Over two thousand years ago, these were thought to be the Seven Wonders of the World:
    The Pyramids of Egypt
    The Hanging Gardens of Babylon
    The Statue of Zeus at Olympia
    The Temple of Artemis at Ephesus
    The Tomb of Mausolus at Halicarnassus
    The Colossus of Rhodes
    The Pharos of Alexandria

The Seven Wonders of The Middle Ages

Over five hundred years ago, these were thought to be the Seven Wonders of the World:
    The Colosseum in Rome
    The Catacombs of Alexandria
    The Great Wall of China

Stonehenge
The Leaning Tower of Pisa
The Porcelain Tower of Nankin
The Mosque of Saint Sophia at Constantinople

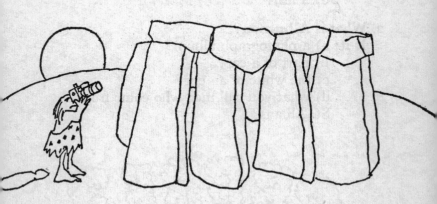

The Seven Wonders of The Modern World

There isn't an 'official' list of the Seven Wonders of
the Modern World, so why don't you make one up?
Here are seven suggestions. How many of them would
you include in *your* list?

The Empire State Building in New York
The Post Office Tower in London
Disneyland in California
The Eiffel Tower in Paris
The Cape Canaveral Space Centre in Florida
The Lake Ponchartrain Causeway in Louisiana
The Blackpool Tower and Illuminations

Words! Words! Words!

1. What is a **Grebe**?
   Is it: a) a bird?
         b) a fat person?
         c) a worm?
         d) a fish?

2. What is **Albumen**?
   Is it: a) a photograph album?
         b) part of a car?
         c) the white of an egg?
         d) what you call men who come from
   St. Albans?

3. What is a **Foxtrot**?
   Is it: a) a race for foxes?
   　　　 b) a fur coat?
   　　　 c) a disease?
   　　　 d) a dance?

4. What is a **Musket**?
   Is it: a) a kind of smell?
   　　　 b) a kind of gun?
   　　　 c) a kind of picnic?
   　　　 d) a kind of poison?

5. What is a **Portmanteau**?
   Is it: a) a suitcase?
   　　　 b) a coathanger?
   　　　 c) a seaside town?
   　　　 d) a drink?

6. What is an **Apothecary**?
   Is it: a) a saint?
   　　　 b) a bee-keeper?
   　　　 c) a chemist?
   　　　 d) an airline pilot?

7. What is a **Lime**?
   Is it: a) a fruit?
   　　　 b) a foreigner?
   　　　 c) a nautical term?
   　　　 d) a spider?

8. What is a **Pedagogue**?
   Is it: a) a footstool?
   b) a tooth-ache?
   c) a musical instrument?
   d) a teacher?

9. What is a **Sapling**?
   Is it: a) a muscle in the leg?
   b) a young tree?
   c) a party game?
   d) a Chinese duck?

10. What is a **Quinquagenarian**?
    Is it: a) someone who is five years old?
    b) someone who is fifty years old?
    c) someone who is seventy-five years old?
    d) someone who lived 500 years ago?

(The answers are on page 115)

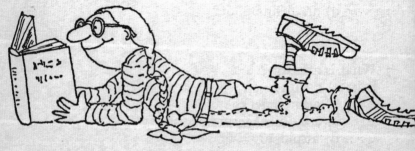

Verbiage

A boy who swims may say he swum,
But milk is skimmed and seldom skum,
And nails you trim, they are not trum.
When words you speak, these words are spoken,
But a nose is tweaked and can't be twoken,
And what you seek is seldom soken.
If we forget then we've forgotten,
But things we wet are never wotten,
And houses let cannot be lotten.
The goods one sells are always sold,
But fears dispelled are not dispold.
And what you smell is never smold.
When young a top you oft saw spun,
But did you see a grin e'er grun,
Or a potato nearly skun?

The Cowboy Maze

(The solution is on page 123)

The Indian Maze

(The solution is on page 124)

Who Said It?

1. Who said:
   'England expects every man will do his duty.'?
   Was it:
   a) Winston Churchill?
   b) The Duke of Wellington?
   c) Admiral Nelson?
   d) Field-Marshal Montgomery?

2. Who said:I
   'Father, cannot tell a lie.'?
   Was it:
   a) Richard Nixon?
   b) Richard III?
   c) George Best?
   d) George Washington?

3. Who said:
   'Let not poor Nelly starve.'?
   Was it:
   a) Charles I?
   b) Charles II?
   c) James I?
   d) James II?

4. Who said:
'Never in the field of human conflict was so much owed by so many to so few.'?
Was it:
a) Adolf Hitler?
b) Benito Mussolini?
c) Winston Churchill?
d) Harold Wilson?

5. Who said:
'England is a nation of shopkeepers.'?
Was it:
a) Queen Victoria?
b) The Emperor Napoleon?
c) King Canute?
d) King Kong?

6. Who said:
   'Let them eat cake!'?
   Was it:
   a) Lady Godiva?
   b) Enid Blyton?
   c) Marie-Antoinette?
   d) Lady Jane Grey?

7. Who said:
   'Ask not what your country can do for you; ask
   what you can do for your country.'?
   Was it:
   a) President Abraham Lincoln?
   b) President Gerald Ford?
   c) President Dwight Eisenhower?
   d) President John Kennedy?

8. Who said:
   'I came, I saw, I conquered.'?
   Was it:
   a) Cleopatra?
   b) Hannibal?
   c) Julius Caesar?
   d) Mark Antony?

(The answers are on page 115)

Mad Tea-party

If your mother's always complaining that she hasn't got time to make tea for you *and* all your friends, tell her not to worry. If she makes enough tea just for you, that's okay. All you and your friends have to do is start at your house, share the tea-for-one between all of you, then move on to someone else's house, share his tea, then move on again and share the third friend's tea and so on. By the end of the afternoon you will all have eaten one complete tea, but none of your mothers will have had to do any extra work!

Loony Limerick

There was a young bard of Japan
Whose limericks never would scan;
    When they said it was so,
    He replied, 'Yes, I know,
But I make a point of always trying to get as many
words into the last line as I possibly can!'

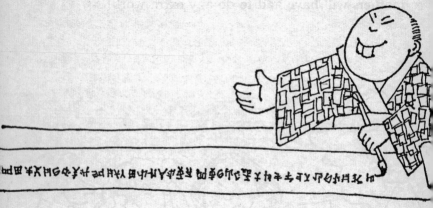

Wonderword

Can you think of a seven-letter word that doesn't
contain any of the five vowels, A, E, I, O, and U?

(The answer is on page 115)

Hotchpotch Hinformation

Gerry Harley, the master barber of Kent, can shave 130 men in 60 minutes!

Commonplace Book

If you don't have a Commonplace Book, now's the time to start one. All you need is a scrapbook, scissors, glue and things to cut out and stick onto the pages. You can put anything you like into your Commonplace Book and you can take as long as you like filling it. Funny headlines from newspapers, cartoons that have made you laugh, jokes you want to remember, the autographs of famous people, recipes for dishes you'd like to learn to cook, a photograph of your favourite football team, the programme from the Christmas pantomime you went to see, a local bus ticket, some snapshots taken on your last holiday, useful telephone numbers, a list of your favourite books ... a Commonplace Book is a book where you can put anything you like that interests *you*. You don't have to include anything you don't want to and, what's more, you don't have to show your Commonplace Book to anyone. It's special. It's secret. And it's all yours.

Century

Here's a game for two players that isn't really a game at all – because there's a trick to it and once you know the trick you are almost certain to win! The idea is to be the first player to reach 100, starting at 0 and counting in turns, adding any number from 1 to 10 on your turn. In order to win, you have simply to be the first player to reach 89, because your opponent will then have to choose a number between 90 and 99, leaving you to reach 100 on your next turn. To make sure you're the first to reach 89, you must be the first to reach 78. And to be first at 78, you must be first at 67. And to be first at 67, you must be first at 56. And so on right back down the line. If you're the first to reach 45, 34, 23, 12 and 1, and you keep your wits about you, you should win the game every time.

If it's your opponent's turn to start and he begins with 1, you can't be certain of victory, but unless he knows the way the system works, the chances are you'll be able to reach one of the all-important key numbers later in the game. In fact, if you suspect that your opponent may be catching on to how you do it, take a risk and choose the numbers at random until you get nearer your century. Providing you're the one who gets to 89, all's well.

Loony Limerick

There once was a man of Bengal
Who was asked to a Fancy Dress Ball.
   He muttered, 'I'll risk it
   And go as a biscuit.'
But the dog ate him up in the hall!

Hotchpotch Crossword – the Not-So-Easy One

All the clues are the dictionary definitions of the words you're looking for.

Clues Across
1. A small crawling creature that will develop into a butterfly or moth.
4. Upper limb of human body from shoulder to hand.
5. Public house for the lodging of travellers.
7. What you have when you are famous.
8. The opposite of over.
10. The opposite of even.
11. The first card in the pack.
13. A vision, series of pictures or events, presented to a sleeping person.
15. Sacred, devoted to God, as in the —— Ghost.
16. The past of eat.
18. A four-winged stinging insect that produces wax and honey.
19. Circuitous roads where all the traffic has to follow a circular course.

Clues Down
1. A large four-wheeled and usually four-horsed carriage; also the name for the trainer of an athletic team.
2. Thin piece of metal with a sharp point at one end and a flattened head at the other used for fastening together materials.
3. A round-up of cattle on an American range or an exhibition of cowboys' skill.
6. An American expression meaning chum, mate, pal, friend.

7. A case or border for enclosing a picture.
9. A female deer, hare or rabbit.
12. The possessive case of they, as 'his' is the possessive case of 'he'.
14. A lady's frock or gown.
17. A shrub grown in India, China and elsewhere, whose dried leaves are used to prepare a drink.

(The answers are on page 116)

Confucius He Say

K'ung-tse was a great and famous Chinese philosopher who lived some 2,500 years ago. We know him as Confucius, but we don't know much about what he really thought and said. Not put off by a lack of facts, we've invented a few of the things the great man *might* have said:

Confucius he say . . .

. . . man who live in glass house should undress in the basement!

Confucius he say . . .

. . . if God had meant us to fly he'd have sent us the tickets!

Confucius he say . . .

. . . scientist who falls into bath of acid getting too absorbed in his work!

Top Tongues

Here is a list of the world's main languages. They are in the wrong order, so can you put them in the right order, with the most spoken language at the top of the list and the least spoken language at the bottom? And can you work out, to the nearest five million, how many people speak each of these languages?

English
French
German
Italian
Spanish
Portuguese
Polish
Russian
Arabic
Hindi

Bengali
Telegu
Tamil
Urdu
Ukrainian
Malay
Javanese
Korean
Japanese
Mandarin Chinese
Min Chinese
Wu Chinese
Cantonese Chinese

(The answers are on page 116)

Lifeboat Men

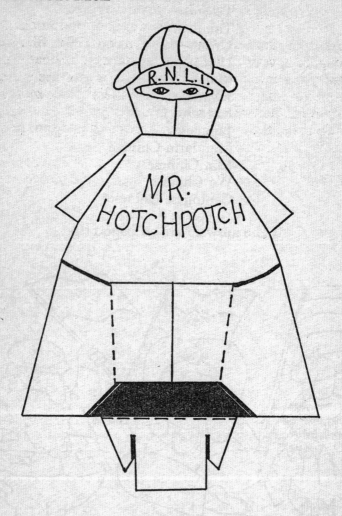

Since it was founded in 1824, the Royal National Lifeboat Institution has saved the lives of almost 100,000 people. With 253 lifeboats stationed all around the British coast, the R.N.L.I. lifeboat men are on duty 24 hours a day, 365 days a year.

One of the R.N.L.I.'s most active supporters is Mrs. Maggie Melbourne of Burton-on-Trent. She has designed a very clever paper model of a lifeboat man that you can cut out, fold into shape and use either as an amusing decoration or as a useful place marker to put on the table at meal times.

To make the model yourself, trace the pattern onto a piece of thin card.

Now cut out the shape, making sure you cut along all the very thick lines and making equally sure you don't cut along any of the other lines.

Now fold the card along the dotted lines and, when you've bent them backwards, slot the side flaps into the bottom flap so that the figure can stand up on its own.

And that's all there is to it. Your model lifeboat man is now ready for action!

(If you would like to know more about the R.N.L.I. and its work, write to the Institution's Headquarters at Claine House, Poole, Dorset.)

Verbs! Verbs! Verbs!

1. What is **to hustle**?
   Is it: a) to push and hurry?
   b) to go to sleep?
   c) to jump high in the air?
   d) to round up cattle?

2. What is **to brawl**?
   Is it: a) to sail a yacht?
   b) to sing loudly?
   c) to fight?
   d) to cook?

3. What is **to gratify**?
   Is it: a) to grate cheese?
   b) to laugh?
   c) to catch a cold?
   d) to please?

4. What is **to munch**?
    Is it: a) to be sick?
          b) to eat?
          c) to spit?
          d) to drink?

5. What is **to repulse**?
    Is it: a) to drive off an attack?
          b) to take a pulse for a second time?
          c) to steal money?
          d) to faint at the sight of blood?

6. What is **to submerge**?
    Is it: a) to climb mountains?
          b) to lift great weights?
          c) to go under water?
          d) to open a bank account?

7. What is **to distort**?
    Is it: a) to make something straight?
          b) to make something die?
          c) to put something out of shape?
          d) to bounce something up and down?

8. What is **to meditate**?
   Is it: a) to visit the Mediterranean?
          b) to administer medicine?
          c) to paint a picture?
          d) to think deeply?

9. What is **to wallop**?
   Is it: a) to serve ice-cream?
          b) to hit someone or something?
          c) to bite someone or something?
          d) to travel by kangaroo?

10. What is **to somnambulate**?
   Is it: a) to call an ambulance?
          b) to try to fly?
          c) to bury someone alive?
          d) to walk in one's sleep?

(The answers are on page 118)

Two Noses

Cross your first finger over your
second finger and rub your crossed
fingers gently up and down the
bridge of your nose. Keep
rubbing for a while and you'll
begin to feel you've got *two*
noses!
Yes, it does sound unlikely,
but try it and you'll find it's
true.

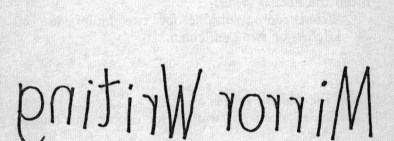

Sit in front of a mirror with a pencil and a large sheet
of paper. Looking into the mirror only, draw a picture
– it can be as simple as you like: a square, a house, a
cat, a tree – and surprise yourself by how difficult it is.
(And if you found it easy, you must have cheated!
Remember: you can only look into the mirror – you
mustn't look down at your hand.)

Odd Ads

From the *Liverpool Echo*:
'Young woman wants washing or cleaning daily.'

From the *New York Times*:
'A toaster for five dollars. It's a gift that every member of the family will enjoy. Automatically burns toast.'

From the *Evening News*:
'Front room, suitable for two ladies, use of kitchen or two gentlemen.'

From the *Nursery World*:
'Experienced girl wanted for cooing and housework.'

From the *Birmingham Post*:
'Lost: large red woman's purse.'

From the *Baltimore Sun*:
'Our stockings and tights are so good that some women wear nothing else.'

The Diver's Maze

(The solution is on page 125)

Talking With the Deaf

If you want to talk to someone who is very hard of hearing or totally deaf, but who can lip-read, there are four golden rules:
1. Face them directly.
2. Don't shout – speak slowly and distinctly.
3. Try to give a visual indication of what you are saying.
4. Use short sentences – each one containing a single thought.

If the person you want to talk to can't lip read, you can use the finger spelling alphabet and spell out what you want to say. It's a very slow process at first, but once you've mastered it, you'll find you can carry on a perfectly normal conversation. Here are the twenty-six letters of the alphabet, plus the shorthand signs for 'Good' and 'Bad':

If you would like to learn more about the problems
of deaf people and feel you want to help them in
some way, write to the Royal National Institute for
the Deaf at 105, Gower Street, London W.C.1.

Here lies till Gabriel's trumpet peal
The bones of Shelby Sharp.
He dozed while holding a steering wheel,
And woke up holding a harp.

Hotchpotch Hinformation

A hypochondriac is someone who always thinks there's something wrong with him and spends all his time worrying about his health. The world's greatest hypochondriac was an Englishman called Samuel Jessop who lived over a hundred and fifty years ago. During his life he drank over 40,000 bottles of medicine and swallowed over 250,000 pills. He died in his sleep at the age of 65.

Grin and Bare It

There once was a man from Blackheath
Who sat on his set of false teeth.
   Said he, with a start,
   'O Lord, bless my heart!
I have bitten myself underneath!'

Thug Twister

Three free thugs set three thugs free.

The Little Dog Laughed Maze

(The solution is on page 126)

A Wonderful Word

Can you think of a word that contains all five vowels (A, E, I, O, U) used only once and in their correct alphabetical order?

To give you a clue, according to the dictionary the word means 'addicted to or marked by pleasantry'.

(The answer is on page 118)

Hotchpotch Hinformation

A loud-mouthed American lady called Mrs. Alton Clapp once managed to talk *non-stop* for 96 hours 45 minutes 11 seconds!

Welsh Rarebit

Some people think that a Welsh Rarebit is a bunny that comes from Cardiff. It isn't. It's one of the world's tastiest snacks and if you don't know how to make it, here's your chance to find out.

Before you start you are going to need:

Half an ounce of butter

Two ounces of grated cheese

A quarter of a teaspoonful of mustard

A pinch of salt

A shake of pepper

A quarter of a tablespoonful of milk

A slice of bread

When you have got all the ingredients – and to make a proper Welsh Rarebit you must have *all* of them – you can begin. Put the butter into a mixing bowl and, with a wooden spoon, stir it until it's soft, then add everything else – except the slice of bread. When you've mixed all the ingredients well, toast the bread. When the bread is toasted, spread on the mixture from the bowl. Now pop the toast under the grill and leave it there for about three minutes. Remove it and eat it. Delicious!

Sporting Tongue-twister

I'm a critical cricket critic.

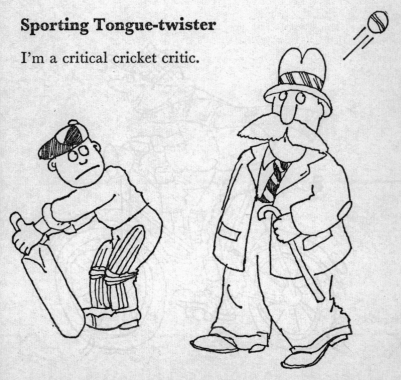

Meet Little Willie

Seventy-five years ago a ghastly little boy called Willie was born somewhere along the East coast of the United States of America. People began to make up rhymes about Willie and his dreadful doings and they've been making up the rhymes ever since. Here are some of the best-loved:

> Little Willie on his bike
> Through the village took a hike.
> Mrs. Johnson blocked the walk –
> She *will* live, but still can't talk.

Willie, hitting at a ball,
Lined one down the school-house hall.
Through the door came Dr. Hill –
Several teeth are missing still.

Willie, as the fire burned low,
Gave it a terrific blow.
Grandpa's beard got in the draught –
Dear me, how the firemen laughed!

Willie, at a passing gent,
Threw a batch of fresh cement,
Crying, 'Wait until you dry –
Then you'll be a real tough guy!'

Willie, with a thirst for gore,
Nailed the baby to the door.
Mother said, with humour quaint –
'Willie, dear, don't spoil the paint.'

A Page of Lightning Sketches

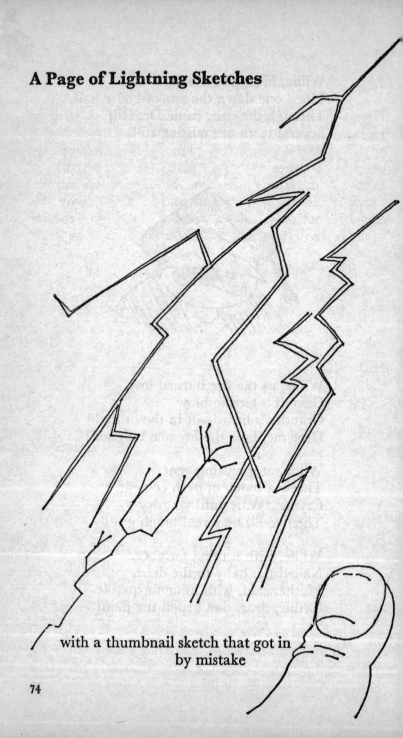

with a thumbnail sketch that got in
by mistake

Egg Roll

Here's a trick to try after breakfast one day when you've had boiled eggs. You need the empty top of an egg-shell and an ordinary china plate. Moisten the plate with water and then place the upturned egg-shell near the edge of the plate. Hold the plate in your hand, incline it slightly and marvel at the way the egg-shell not only slides around the plate but rotates at an incredible speed. With practice, this trick looks very effective and you can even manage several spinning, rolling eggs at the same time.

The Doctors Were Surprised

Mary had a little lamb,
    A lobster and some prunes,
A glass of milk, a piece of pie,
    And then some macaroons;
It made the naughty waiters grin
    To see her order so,
And when they carried Mary out,
    Her face was white as snow.

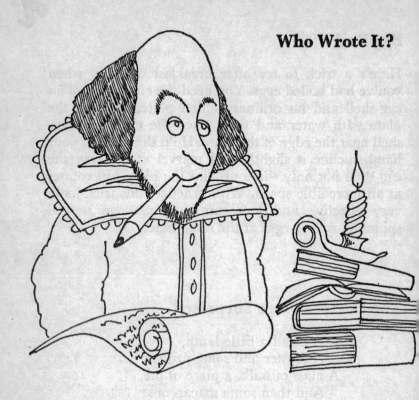

1. Who wrote *Twelfth Night*?
   Was it: Tom Stoppard?
   Charles Dickens?
   William Shakespeare?
   William Wordsworth?

2. Who wrote *Murder at the Vicarage*?
   Was it: Arthur Conan Doyle?
   John Buchan?
   Agatha Christie?
   Ngaio Marsh?

3. Who wrote *Good Companions*?
   Was it: I. Asimov?
             J. B. Priestley?
             R. D. Blackmore?
             E. Nesbit?

4. Who wrote *Androcles and the Lion*?
   Was it: William Makepiece Thackeray?
             Henry Wadsworth Longfellow?
             George Bernard Shaw?
             Ian Fleming?

5. Who wrote *Ode to a Nightingale*?
   Was it: John Keats?
             Oscar Wilde?
             John Betjeman?
             Donny Osmond?

6. Who wrote *Watership Down*?
   Was it: Richard Gordon?
             Harold Pinter?
             James Herriot?
             Richard Adams?

(The answers are on page 118)

Hotchpotch Hilarity

How long will an eight-day clock run without winding?

It won't run at all without winding!

Knowing Your Place

Everyone knows that the Queen is Head of State and, as Sovereign, counts as the country's Top Person. But who comes next in the official pecking order? Prince Philip? Right. And after him? Prince Charles? Right again. But now it begins to get a bit more complicated – unless, of course, you happen to know the official 'Order of Precedence in England' off by heart. If you do, then you'll know who ranks over who If you don't, never fear, *Hotchpotch* is here!

It's well worth studying the 'Order of Precedence', just in case you get invited to Prince Charles' wedding

or the next coronation. It's always nice to know where you're supposed to be standing in the queue.

(If you happen to be a girl you may be a bit surprised to see that everyone in the Order of Precedence is male – except, of course, for the Queen! This is because the people who make up these things are frightfully old-fashioned and foolish. If you ask them where women come in the Order of Precedence this is what they'll tell you: 'Women take the same rank as their husbands or as their eldest brothers, but the daughter of a peer marrying a commoner retains her own title as Lady or Honourable. Daughters of peers rank next immediately after the wives of their elder brothers and before their younger brothers' wives. Daughters of peers marrying peers of lower degree take the same order of precedency as that of their husbands; thus the daughter of a duke marrying a baron becomes of the rank of baroness, while her sisters married to commoners retain their rank and take precedence over the baroness. Merely official rank on the husband's part does not give any similar precedence to the wife.' Whatever it's supposed to mean, it *sounds* pretty unfair!)

THE SOVEREIGN
PRINCE PHILIP
PRINCE CHARLES
PRINCE ANDREW
PRINCE EDWARD
THE ARCHBISHOP
  OF CANTERBURY

THE LORD HIGH CHANCELLOR
THE ARCHBISHOP OF YORK
THE PRIME MINISTER
THE LORD PRESIDENT OF THE COUNCIL
THE SPEAKER OF THE HOUSE OF COMMONS
THE LORD PRIVY SEAL
THE HIGH COMMISSIONERS OF COMMONWEALTH
    COUNTRIES AND THE AMBASSADORS OF FOREIGN
    STATES
DUKES, ACCORDING TO THEIR PATENTS OF CREATION,
    OF ENGLAND, OF SCOTLAND, OF GREAT BRITAIN,

OF IRELAND AND THOSE CREATED SINCE THE UNION
MINISTERS AND ENVOYS
ELDEST SONS OF DUKES OF BLOOD ROYAL
MARQUESSES IN THE SAME ORDER AS DUKES
DUKES' ELDEST SONS
EARLS IN THE SAME ORDER AS DUKES
YOUNGER SONS OF DUKES OF BLOOD ROYAL
MARQUESSES' ELDEST SONS
DUKES' YOUNGER SONS
VISCOUNTS IN THE SAME ORDER AS DUKES
EARLS' ELDEST SONS
MARQUESSES' YOUNGER SONS
THE BISHOPS OF LONDON, DURHAM AND WINCHESTER
ALL OTHER ENGLISH BISHOPS, ACCORDING TO THEIR
    SENIORITY OF CONSECRATION
SECRETARIES OF STATE, IF OF THE DEGREE OF A BARON
BARONS, IN THE SAME ORDER AS DUKES
THE TREASURER OF HER MAJESTY'S
    HOUSEHOLD
THE COMPTROLLER OF H.M.'S HOUSEHOLD

THE VICE-CHAMBERLAIN OF H.M.'S HOUSEHOLD
SECRETARIES OF STATE UNDER THE DEGREE OF BARON
VISCOUNT'S ELDEST SONS
EARLS' YOUNGER SONS
BARONS' ELDEST SONS
KNIGHTS OF THE GARTER, IF COMMONERS
PRIVY COUNCILLORS, IF OF NO HIGHER RANK
THE CHANCELLOR OF THE EXCHEQUER
THE CHANCELLOR OF THE DUCHY OF LANCASTER
THE LORD CHIEF JUSTICE OF ENGLAND
THE MASTER OF THE ROLLS
THE PRESIDENT OF THE PROBATE COURT
THE LORDS JUSTICES OF APPEAL
THE JUDGES OF THE HIGH COURT
THE VICE-CHANCELLOR OF COUNTY PALATINE OF
    LANCASTER
VISCOUNTS' YOUNGER SONS
BARONS' YOUNGER SONS
SONS OF LIFE PEERS
BARONETS OF EITHER KINGDOM, ACCORDING TO DATE OF
    PATENTS
KNIGHTS OF THE THISTLE, IF COMMONERS
KNIGHTS GRAND CROSS OF THE BATH
MEMBERS OF THE ORDER OF MERIT
KNIGHTS GRAND COMMANDERS OF THE STAR OF INDIA

KNIGHTS GRAND CROSS OF ST. MICHAEL AND ST. GEORGE

KNIGHTS GRAND COMMANDERS OF THE INDIAN EMPIRE

KNIGHTS GRAND CROSS OF THE ROYAL VICTORIAN ORDER

KNIGHTS GRAND CROSS OF THE ORDER OF THE BRITISH
EMPIRE

COMPANIONS OF HONOUR

KNIGHTS COMMANDERS OF THE ABOVE ORDERS

KNIGHTS BACHELOR

OFFICIAL REFEREES OF THE SUPREME COURT

JUDGES OF COUNTY COURTS AND JUDGES OF THE
MAYOR'S AND CITY OF LONDON COURT

COMPANIONS AND COMMANDERS

ELDEST SONS OF YOUNGEST SONS OF PEERS

BARONETS' ELDEST SONS

ELDEST SONS OF KNIGHTS IN THE SAME ORDER AS THEIR
FATHERS

MEMBERS OF THE ROYAL VICTORIAN ORDER (5TH CLASS)

MEMBERS OF THE ORDER OF THE BRITISH EMPIRE

YOUNGER SONS OF THE YOUNGER SONS OF PEERS

BARONETS' YOUNGER SONS

YOUNGER SONS OF KNIGHTS IN THE SAME ORDER AS
THEIR FATHERS

NAVAL, MILITARY, AIR AND OTHER ESQUIRES BY OFFICE

THE REST OF US!

That's Showbiz!

1. What is the name of the first British actor to have been made a Lord?
   Is it: Henry Irving?
   　　　Laurence Olivier?
   　　　Michael Caine?
   　　　Michael Crawford?

2. What is the name of the great American tap dancer who starred in many Hollywood musicals with Ginger Rogers?
   Is it: Bing Crosby?
   　　　Gene Kelly
   　　　Fred Astaire?
   　　　Lionel Blair?

3. Eric Bartholomew and Ernest Wiseman are a famous British comedy duo. By what names are they better known?
Are they: Flanders and Swann?
Derry and Toms?
Mike and Bernie Winters?
Morecambe and Wise?

4. Who has won more Oscars than anyone else in the history of the cinema?
Is it: Walt Disney?
Elizabeth Taylor?
Bob Hope?
Hayley Mills?

5. Who was Arthur Stanley Jefferson's screen partner in the early days of silent comedy films?
Was it: Buster Keaton?
Oliver Hardy?
Harold Lloyd?
Charlie Chaplin?

6. In the long-running television series *Coronation Street* Violet Carson plays an important part.
   Is it: Miss Marple?
   Florence Nightingale?
   Ena Sharples?
   Elizabeth I?

7. She has been married to Conrad Hilton, Michael Wilding, Michael Todd, Eddie Fisher and Richard Burton. What's her name?
   Is it: Noel Gordon?
   Lulu?
   Elizabeth Taylor?
   Zsa Zsa Gabor?

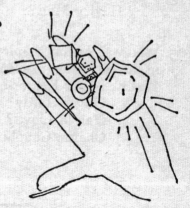

8. He is the lead singer in a successful pop group called the Rolling Stones. What's his name?
   Is it: Elton John?
   Garry Glitter?
   Tom Jones?
   Mick Jagger?

9. Ehrich Weiss, who lived from 1873 to 1926, was probably the greatest escapologist and magician the world has known. By what name was he better known?

Was it: David Nixon?
Evel Knievel?
Harry Houdini?
Mr. Fixit?

10. Sooty and Sweep are glove puppets created and manipulated by who?

Is it: Harry Lauder?
Harry Worth?
Harry Andrews?
Harry Corbett?

Hotchpotch Hinformation

The world's largest living creature is the Blue Whale (or *balaenoptera musculus*) which can grow to be 100 feet long. And the smallest is a tiny organism known as *mycoplasma laidlawii* whose diameter can be as minute as 0·000004 of an inch.

Hotchpotch Hilarity

What is always coming, but never arrives?

Tomorrow!

How do you keep food in an empty stomach?

Bolt it down!

What time is it when the clock strikes thirteen?

Time to have it mended!

Matchbox Boxing Match

This is a tough fight for two players, but it's a safe one to try because nobody gets hurt. You and your opponent stand face to face, with your right arms outstretched and your left arms firmly tucked behind your backs. A matchbox is placed on the back of each of the right hands. On the command 'Go!' the fight begins and the aim of the game is to knock the matchbox off your opponent's right hand without letting him knock your matchbox off yours. The first player whose matchbox bites the dust is the loser.

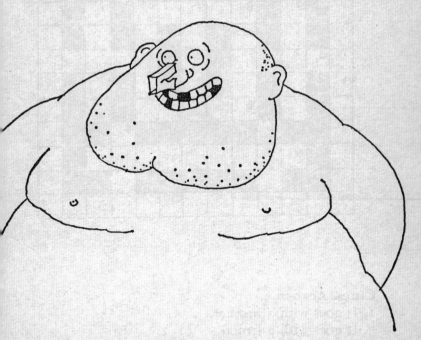

Hotchpotch Crossword –

the Tough One

Clues Across
1. It goes with a brother.
3. It goes with a lemon.
6. It goes with a trumpet.
8. The opposite of an exit.
12. A male red deer.

13. The opposite of hot.
16. If you add a 'T' to the opposite of odd you get a special occasion.
19. No city is complete without this kind of church.
20. The enemy of Saint George.
21. In the game of chess this is also called a rook.

Clues Down

1. The opposite of sunrise.
2. In the school year there are usually three of these.
4. Here's a word that begins and ends with the same letter and means a piece of ground. If you're in a part of the world you don't know, you might say you were in a 'strange ——'.
5. The Romans would have written it like this: XI.
7. 'Tee-hee-hee! You can't —— me!'
8. Once upon a time there was a boys' comic named after this large bird of prey.
9. This is part of an animal's stomach, but it's a word we also use to describe something someone's said when we think it's rubbish.
10. A sailing ship.
11. She put the kettle on.
14. An unusual and exotic flower.
15. Another word for 'take away'.
17. If you burst a balloon this is what you'll hear.
18. The opposite of lad.

(The answers are on page 120)

The Lighthouse Maze

(The solution is on page 127)

The Golliwog Maze

(The solution is on page 128)

Loony Limerick

There was a young man of Devizes
Whose ears were of different sizes.
   The one that was small
   Was no use at all,
But the other won several prizes!

Hotchpotch Hinformation

Those who enjoy doing press-ups might like to rise to the challenge of breaking the world press-ups record. In 1965 a sixteen year-old American called Chick Linster did 6,006 press-ups in 3 hours 54 minutes. Beat that!

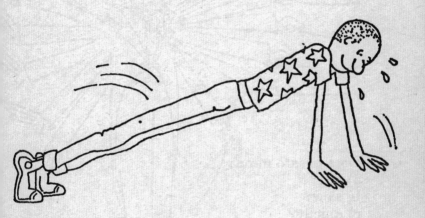

Paper Chase

Stand on a chair and, from your great height, drop a single sheet of paper. Get someone to stand on the floor in front of you and challenge him to catch the piece of paper between his finger and thumb as it floats towards the ground. It sounds very easy, doesn't it? Well, try it, and you'll find that nine times out of ten, the paper will fall to the ground without being caught.

Musical Meanings

Here are some well-known musical terms. All you've got to do is work out their meanings.

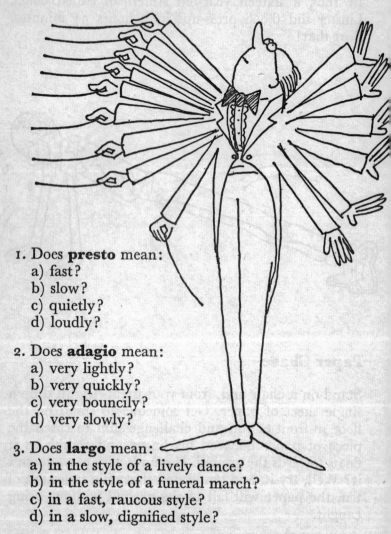

1. Does **presto** mean:
   a) fast?
   b) slow?
   c) quietly?
   d) loudly?

2. Does **adagio** mean:
   a) very lightly?
   b) very quickly?
   c) very bouncily?
   d) very slowly?

3. Does **largo** mean:
   a) in the style of a lively dance?
   b) in the style of a funeral march?
   c) in a fast, raucous style?
   d) in a slow, dignified style?

4. Does **fortissimo** mean:
   a) very fast?
   b) very slow?
   c) very loud?
   d) very soft?

5. Does **dolce** mean:
   a) angrily?
   b) sorrowfully?
   c) sweetly?
   d) tearfully?

6. Does **crescendo** mean:
   a) singing very loudly?
   b) decreasing the volume slowly?
   c) singing very softly?
   d) increasing the volume slowly?

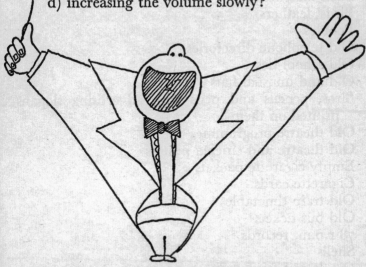

(The answers are on page 120)

Collector's Instinct

It's something we've almost all got: the urge to build a collection, to choose something that interests us and really do all we can to find as many examples of it as we can. We can't all collect oil paintings or racehorses, but we can all collect *something*. If you haven't yet started a collection, why not try? You may think there's not much to collect – just stamps and old coins – but if you do think that, you're wrong. There are masses of amazing things that people can collect and most of them cost next-to-nothing. Here are a few ideas to get you going:

Beer mats
Wrappers that go round sugar lumps
Wrappers that go round tins of food
Matchboxes
Book matches
Birds' feathers
Pebbles
Old telephone directories
Old school ties
Old and unusual hats
Biros, pencils and pens with advertising slogans
    printed on them
Old theatre programmes
Old theatre and cinema posters
Empty cigarette packets
Cigarette cards
Old train timetables
Old bus tickets
78 r.p.m. records
Shells
Catalogues from stores

Paper bags with different advertising slogans on them
Postcards
Examples of old handwriting
Old and unusual buttons
Carousel books by Gyles Brandreth

Definitions from a Daft Dictionary

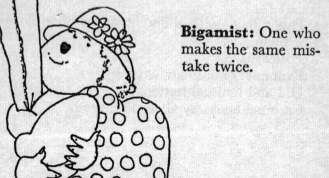

Actor: A man who tries to be everything but himself.

Adult: A person who has stopped growing at both ends and started growing in the middle.

Advertising: That which makes you think you've longed for something all your life when you've never even heard of it before.

Bigamist: One who makes the same mistake twice.

Bores: People who insist on talking about themselves when you want to talk about yourself.

Criminal: One who gets caught.

Dachshund: An animal that's half-a-dog high by a dog-and-a-half long.

Earth: A solid substance, much sought after by the sea-sick.

Hospitals: Places where people who are run down wind up.

Hug: A roundabout way of expressing affection.

Laundry: A place where clothes are mangled.

Nudist: A person who goes around coatless and jacketless and shirtless and vestless – and wears trousers to match!

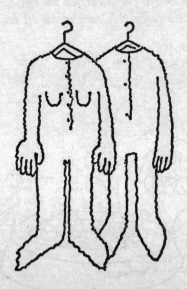

Here *lie* I
Bereft of breath
Because a cough carried me off,
Then a coffin they carried me off in.

When Was That?

1. Sir Alexander Fleming discovered penicillin, the first 'antibiotic'. When was that?
   Was it in: 1759?
   1891?
   1928?
   1947?

2. Guy Fawkes was the leader of the famous Gunpowder Plot. When was that?
   Was it in: 1605?
   1776?
   1812?
   1914?

3. The Prince Regent became King George IV on the death of George III. When was that?
   Was it in: 1066?
   1314?
   1616?
   1820?

4. When East Germany sealed the border between East and West Berlin, the Berlin Wall was built. When was that?
   Was it in: 1899?
   1919?
   1951?
   1961?

5. C. S. Rolls met Henry Royce and formed a company to make motor cars. When was that?
Was it in: 1850?
1906?
1930?
1956?

6. The Roman Emperor, Julius Caesar, was murdered by a group of conspirators led by Brutus and Cassius. When was that?
Was it in: 44 BC*?
44 AD*?
1444?
1944?

* BC stands for 'Before Christ' and the Year 1 is supposed to mark the year in which Jesus was born. In fact, he was probably born four years earlier, in 4 BC. AD stands for 'Anno Domini' meaning 'the year of Our Lord', so all the years after Year 1 are AD and all the years before are BC.

7. Yuri Gagarin was the first man in space when he orbited the earth for 1 hour 48 minutes in a five-ton Russian spaceship called Vostok. When was that?
   Was it in: 1908?
   1929?
   1961?
   1972?

8. The English fleet defeated the Spanish Armada sent against England by Philip II of Spain. When was that?
   Was it in: 1400?
   1588?
   1695?
   1740?

9. An Englishman called Christopher Cockerell invented the Hovercraft. When was that?
   Was it in: 1882?
   1936?
   1959?
   1974?

10. At the time of her death Queen Victoria had reigned longer than any other British monarch. When was that?
    Was it in: 1507?
    1679?
    1804?
    1901?

11. President Abraham Lincoln was assassinated at the theatre. When was that?
Was it in: 1775?
1865?
1945?
1960?

12. President John Kennedy was assassinated in Dallas, Texas. When was that?
Was it in: 1962?
1963?
1964?
1965?

(The answers are on page 121)

Weak Word

Can you think of a fifteen-letter word in which the only vowel is the letter E which is used three times in the word?

(The answer is on page 122)

Hotchpotch Hinformation

The elephant has 40,000 muscles in its trunk – but not a single bone.

Initiative Test

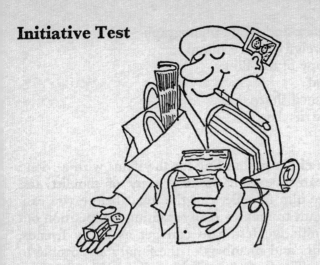

If you like a challenge, this is the game for you. In the next three hours, find, collect and bring back to base the following twenty items:

1. A copy of the local newspaper.
2. A used bus ticket.
3. A 1p coin dated 1976
4. The name of the local Station Master
5. A copy of the Complete Works of William Shakespeare
6. A piece of string one foot long
7. A pebble
8. A button
9. A gold milk-bottle top.
10. The telephone number of the local police station
11. A Post Office telegram form
12. A potato crisp
13. A packet of book-matches
14. A drinking straw

15. A black-and-white photograph
16. A foreign postage stamp
17. A copy of the Bible
18. A leaf
19. A pencil sharpener
20. A carrier bag

You can either go hunting for the items with a friend *or* you can give your friend a copy of the list and challenge him to collect all the items before you can. If you want to make a really exciting competition out of the initiative test, you can get as many friends, neighbours and members of the family as possible to take part. The first player back to base with all twenty items is the winner.

Home Truths

> Women's faults are many,
> 　　Men have only two:
> Everything they say,
> 　　And everything they do!

Broken Nose

If anyone in your family is squeamish and you fancy giving them a bit of a fright, why not break your own nose in front of their very eyes. As they hear it crack, they'll flinch or even faint – while you fall about helpless with laughter!

All you have to do is place the palms of your hands together and grip your nose between your two forefingers. Now put the thumbnail of either hand behind your upper front teeth and as you twist your nose from side to side with your forefingers, you click your thumbnail on your teeth. It sounds very nasty, but it feels rather nice.

Composers' Corner

Here, listed in the order of their birth, are the names of some of the world's greatest and most famous composers. In among the real names, dates and nationalities are five phoneys. Can you spot them?

George Friedrich Handel (1685–1759) German
Johann Sebastian Bach (1685–1750) German
Franz Joseph Haydn (1732–1809) Austrian
Rudolph Von Smettow (1740–1801) German
Wolfgang Amadeus Mozart (1756–1791) Austrian
Hector Adolph Buzzi (1769–1812) Swiss
Ludwig Van Beethoven (1770–1827) German
Gioacchino Rossini (1792–1868) Italian
Franz Peter Schubert (1797–1828) Austrian
Mikhail Ivanovitch Glinka (1804–1857) Russian
Frederic Chopin (1810–1849) Polish

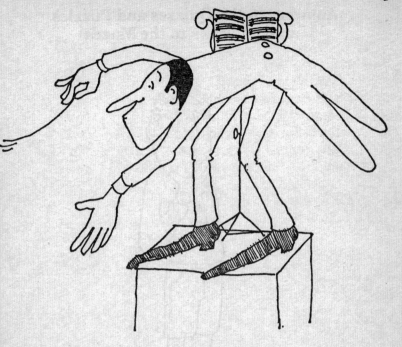

Franz Liszt (1811–1886) Hungarian
Richard Wagner (1813–1883) German
Giuseppe Pizza (1813–1901) Italian
Johannes Brahms (1833–1897) German
Georges Bizet (1838–1875) French
Peter Ilyich Tchaikovsky (1840–1893) Russian
Arthur Sullivan (1842–1900) English
Igor Plinplonski (1850–1937) Russian
Gustav Mahler (1860–1911) Austrian
Richard Strauss (1864–1949) German
Kurt Barsolova (1864–1956) Hungarian
Jean Sibelius (1865–1957) Finnish

(The answers are on page 122)

Answers to the Quizzes and Puzzles and Solutions to the Mazes

Anniversary Quiz

One year	=	Cotton
Two years	=	Paper
Three years	=	Leather
Four years	=	Silk
Five years	=	Wooden
Six years	=	Sweets
Seven years	=	Woollen
Eight years	=	Bronze
Nine years	=	Pottery
Ten years	=	Tin
Fifteen years	=	Crystal
Twenty years	=	China
Thirty years	=	Pearl
Thirty-five years	=	Coral
Forty years	=	Ruby
Forty-five years	=	Sapphire
Fifty-five years	=	Emerald

Hotchpotch Crossword – the Easy One

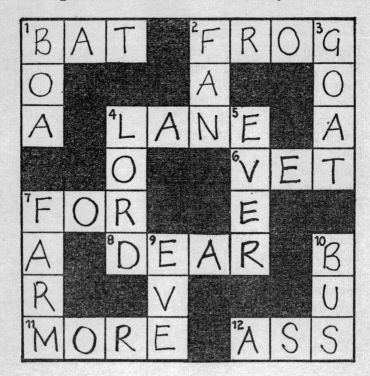

Where Will You Find It?

1. Nigeria
2. Pakistan
3. Saudi Arabia
4. England
5. Switzerland
6. Yugoslavia

Words! Words! Words!

1. A **Grebe** is a bird
2. **Albumen** is the white of an egg
3. A **Foxtrot** is a dance
4. A **Musket** is a kind of gun
5. A **Portmanteau** is a suitcase
6. An **Apothecary** is a chemist
7. A **Lime** is a fruit
8. A **Pedagogue** is a teacher
9. A **Sapling** is a young tree
10. A **Quinquagenarian** is someone who is fifty years old.

Who Said It?

1) Admiral Nelson
2) George Washington
3) Charles II
4) Winston Churchill
5) The Emperor Napoleon
6) Marie-Antoinette
7) President John Kennedy
8) Julius Caesar

Wonderword

Rhythms

Hotchpotch Crossword – the Not-So-Easy-One

C	A	T	E	R	P	I	L	L	A	R
O					I					O
A	R	M		I	N	N				D
C			B				F	A	M	E
H			U	N	D	E	R			O
	O	D	D				A	C	E	
T			D	R	E	A	M			D
H	O	L	Y			E				R
E				A	T	E		B	E	E
I				E						S
R	O	U	N	D	A	B	O	U	T	S

Top Tongues

1. Mandarin Chinese — 493 million speakers
2. English — 291 ,, ,,
3. Russian — 167 ,, ,,
4. Hindi — 162 ,, ,,
5. Spanish — 155 ,, ,,
6. German — 123 ,, ,,

7. Japanese	98 million speakers	
8. Bengali	85 „	„
9. Arabic	82 „	„
10. Portuguese	80 „	„
11. French	73 „	„
12. Malay	71 „	„
13. Italian	58 „	„
14. Urdu	54 „	„
15. Cantonese Chinese	45 „	„
16. Javanese	42 „	„
17. Ukrainian	41 „	„
18. Telegu	40 „	„
19. Wu Chinese	39 „	„
20. Tamil	37 „	„
21. Min Chinese	36 „	„
22. Korean	35 „	„
23. Polish	34 „	„

Verbs! Verbs! Verbs!

1. **To hustle** is to push and hurry
2. **To brawl** is to fight
3. **To gratify** is to please
4. **To munch** is to eat
5. **To repulse** is to drive off an attack
6. **To submerge** is to go under water
7. **To distort** is to put something out of shape
8. **To meditate** is to think deeply
9. **To wallop** is to hit someone or something
10. **To somnambulate** is to walk in one's sleep

A Wonderful Word

Facetious

Who Wrote It?

1. William Shakespeare.
2. Agatha Christie.
3. J. B. Priestley.
4. George Bernard Shaw.
5. John Keats.
6. Richard Adams.

That's Showbiz!

1. Laurence Olivier.
2. Fred Astaire.
3. Morecambe and Wise.
4. Walt Disney.
5. Oliver Hardy.
6. Ena Sharples.
7. Elizabeth Taylor.
8. Mick Jagger.
9. Harry Houdini.
10. Harry Corbett.

Hotchpotch Crossword – the Tough One

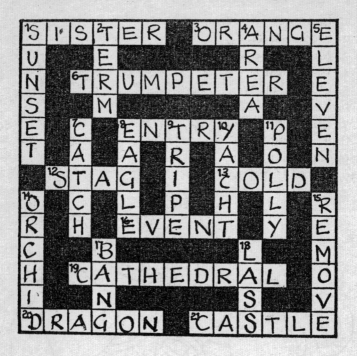

Musical Meanings

1. **Presto** means fast.
2. **Adagio** means very slowly.
3. **Largo** means in a slow, dignified style.
4. **Fortissimo** means very loud.
5. **Dolce** means sweetly.
6. **Crescendo** means increasing the volume slowly.

When Was That?

1. 1928.
2. 1605.
3. 1820.
4. 1961.
5. 1906.
6. 44 BC.
7. 1961.
8. 1588.
9. 1959.
10. 1901.
11. 1865.
12. 1963.

Weak Word

Strengthlessness

Composers' Corner

These are the five phoneys:
Rudolph Von Smettow
Hector Adolph Buzzi
Giuseppe Pizza
Igor Plinplonski
Kurt Barsolova

The Cowboy Maze

The Indian Maze

The Diver's Maze

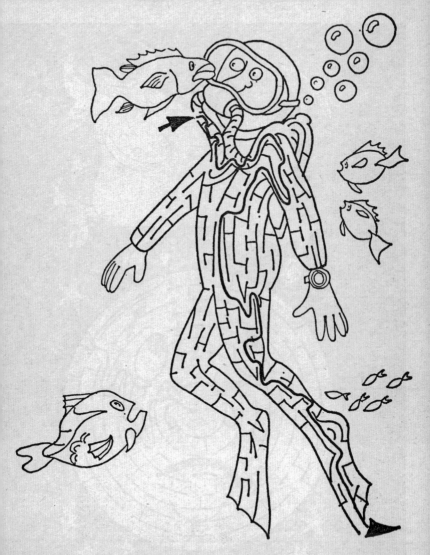

The Little Dog Laughed Maze

The Lighthouse Maze

The Golliwog Maze